THE CURIOUS THING

ALSO BY SANDRA LIM

Loveliest Grotesque

The Wilderness

THE
CURIOUS
THING

POEMS

Sandra Lim

W. W. NORTON & COMPANY
Independent Publishers Since 1923

For information about permission to reproduce selections from this book, write to
Permissions, W. W. Norton & Company, Inc., 500 Fifth Avenue, New York, NY 10110

For information about special discounts for bulk purchases, please contact
W. W. Norton Special Sales at specialsales@wwnorton.com or 800-233-4830

Manufacturing by Versa Press
Production manager: Julia Druskin

Library of Congress Cataloging-in-Publication Data
Names: Lim, Sandra, author.
Title: The curious thing : poems / Sandra Lim.
Description: First Edition. | New York, NY : W. W. Norton & Company, [2021]
Identifiers: LCCN 2021021177 | ISBN 9780393867893 (hardcover) |
ISBN 9780393867909 (epub)
Subjects: LCGFT: Poetry.
Classification: LCC PS3612.I467 C87 2021 | DDC 811/.6—dc23
LC record available at https://lccn.loc.gov/2021021177

W. W. Norton & Company, Inc., 500 Fifth Avenue, New York, N.Y. 10110
www.wwnorton.com

W. W. Norton & Company Ltd., 15 Carlisle Street, London W1D 3BS

1 2 3 4 5 6 7 8 9 0

You must let yourself go along in life like a cork in the current of a stream.
— PIERRE-AUGUSTE RENOIR

· less interested in figurative lang.
    · deliberatively flattening lang + any
  brisking non endings
· passivity v. agency
    · suspicion of engaging w/ abstraction

CONTENTS

THE CURIOUS THING

THE PROTAGONISTS

At one time,
I asked for everything—

When I saw how my love was squandered,
I would secrete venom.

But now I sing of the fat, sleepy
little censor
who has replaced me, whose disappointments

create the life of the house.
What does the human heart love?
To go, to have so far to go,

in deepest night!

The challenge now
is to convey the supreme gaiety
of the heart:

it is a stone   cork in a stream
flung from a volcano.

CHICAGO

handwritten: sketch of the mind —

handwritten: • tense relationship btn literal — figurative
handwritten: as if always lifting up, grounding the self

I had a little stove, and a wick of wakefulness
in my sleep.

In the mornings, I heard the train roar and go up
into the center of things.

I circulated thoughts like,
I will always be restless for crowds and lights and noise.

I would take long walks and say to no one,
When I was first married . . .

I saw all of Luis Buñuel's films inside of a week:
the darkness was delicious. I could always almost smell it.

I wasn't young, I wasn't old, I was still nibbling
at what lay before me.

And later, when I didn't have the energy to wait out the days
made unalike only by fact of the seasons,

I planned a few things, too.

handwritten: • moving/shifting of pronouns —

SOMETHING MEANS EVERYTHING

I had a long and mysterious fever
when I was four years old. I was in bed for five months.
My mother took the illness
as some obscure anger of mine
that took time to assuage, a root fire underground.
ease
That is what she told me once, anyway.
I think I lived to myself. _strange_
I like to imagine that I was at one time
truly formless and uncaring, only yearning toward
water and sleep, opening and closing.
She said that in my fever, I even spat at her once:
when I looked up into her face, my eyes were plain and bright,
and she thought I was becoming something
that she knew nothing about.
And then it passed. For once, my spirit refuses the effort
of understanding. Of course I could not see what lay
before me, then. I was a child, wasn't I.
I didn't have my heart set on anything. Whereas now,
facts are more solid than I can stand.
I need a few more ideas. A room of one's own is splendid.
You don't know what your story is about _key_
when you begin it. And a love to measure past
and future loves against: the danger may be that it carries
the force of original thought, when in reality,
it is just what you have had with you
all along, the curious thing lying on your heart.
Like that childhood fever, it's private, without account.
I had a dream around that early time, or was it a real episode,
my mother can't remember. I saw the most beautiful

contention of memory — a vision or a dream

young woman on the street, and when she turned to look down and smile
upon me, I saw that she had no teeth at all.
Uncertain, the distortion had stopped in her face.
But it was like a promise, wasn't it, the prediction
of a poisoning of spirit, or its very healing. I am not sure now which.

JEAN RHYS

It's now within
an hour of sundown of a late
November afternoon.

It was a beautiful day,
the cold burned
down any indignation.

What won't degrade:
the sick and distant, or near and black,
bad-natured tides of want.

Jean Rhys is saying
If I could jump out of the window
one bang and I'd be out of it.

It isn't done
to admit to this kind
of need,

but spirit needs a house, x2 opening
and the brief pageant of being
escorted through

the grieving joy of words
set down right. The cold bores her,
oppresses her. Life

comes to bore her. She can strip
a thing down. I want
beauty, she adds. Hear me?

I hear you, Jean. Yours is a voice
disabused; and inside the cold of it,
there's a sort of festival. – pagent

to free
from error

THE IMMORALISTS

In Goethe's famous ballad
a little heath rose tells a rough boy she'll prick him if he picks her,
but he picks her anyway

Look how the erotic imagination
honors you little rose, it runs its kingly grace over you
remorselessly

We go out into the light
of a hot Sunday afternoon; none of us wants to grow old
in a library

CHANSON DOUCE – *a sweet song*

I hold a creamy little baby
to my chest. She assents to my embrace. I inquire
about my species: she has a look
of true, plain being.
She is need itself. Sucking. Crying.
Otherwise, her expression is basically
serious, and the devotion she summons, famously
brutal. Her mother would die for her,
the old, old story.

to compare the stanzas —

Part of me watches the rest of me being
anxious, superior, and invaded
by longing. These rank weeds spring up
beside a curious sense
of sequel. I remember it sharply now: a little
time ago, wishing I had something
new, and the strain of it *wow*
nearly killing me. There was
no deeper meaning.

18

THE FUTURE

Who or what
can beseech you now?

There are no origins
or general principles.

There is only this hole in the earth.

Can you still be afraid
then, for what you don't have,

and what you'll never have?

That despair is like an explosion
of understanding.

It can make you quite careless.

But the pain of not knowing
how to write—

Ah, says Fate, you have a treat coming.
And it was always so.

BOSTON

When I first moved to this city to take a job,
and the snows began to fall, a slow sadness took hold of me.

Someone left a tiny pencil drawing of a sailboat
on the ceiling of my bedroom, and I would stare up at it each night,

thinking that it would eventually stir.
I met someone that first spring, and I didn't love him.

But I very much wanted someone to look at me, ¡ ¡ ¡
in all my youth and feminine momentum.

BLACK BOX

We were in a small, grim café.

She sipped pure black droplets
from a tiny cup.

Make him come back, she said,
her voice like something brought up intact
from the cold center of a lake.

It was the kind of story I like, and I wanted
to get it right, for later:

*relief/ direction
of interior voice*

*• preoccupation w/
how to tell a story,
correctly*

The hot morning in the café,
feeling encroached on by a cloud
of dusty ferns and creepers

and the low earth of duty.

I can't read a book
all the way through, she said,
and most days I'm only unhappy.

My heart is always with the lovers.

THEME AND VARIATION

A frightened happiness went through him

now, and in secret, at the prospect of a different world

with her. He appeared the affronted loner,

but it was she who had never been loved or saved;

her rooms were immaculate.

He found the stars extravagant that winter,

and impossible to resist. Certain conditions prevailed

in his fine mathematical mind: time is fixed,

and ends are certain. Clarity and justice.

For her, every confrontation left a burnt place in creation,

fastening its moment in the ultimate heart

of things. But it kept multiplying what could never take place.

She fretted about all her hope running out, whereas he became

preoccupied with systems. The stars never change

their places, though what potential this afforded, he wondered.

PASTORAL

When you called, I would come running, all my tags jingling.
You'd grab a hank of my hair, and that would block out every thought.

Our bodies swelled and stank in the heat,
and we caved to it all day, under a cloud of flies.

I dreamt of strung pheasants in old paintings, a horse
of thick paste biting my arm. I dreamt of nothing.

Sticky and hungry, we were like bad-tempered children who stay out
too long in the rain. They feel lonely but have no language for it.

You once gashed your head open. My leg twisted beneath me
at a serene new angle. Our greed was largest, and most generous.

With the sun high behind us, we weren't two but four,
our shadows playing ahead of us in the melting summer grasses.

We became almost ugly with use, our questions traveling too fast,
no one stopping to answer. The cat looked into our faces through sleepy slits.

I dreamt that I died. You weren't even very sad: you touched
my face, it was already cold. And cold was beyond understanding.

THE STRONGER

With me, life becomes sweeter,
so she loses some of
the ability to defend herself.
Yet even this gives her a forlorn
sense of satisfaction.
I know it by the distracted
half-smile on her face.
People believe love
can do so much! As when
they talk incessantly
about the weather:
they sound as if they're waiting
for something incredible
to come their way.
Nestled against me,
isn't she a moron of joy.
She loves to tell stories
because they're already finished
by the start of the telling.
Her favorites are driven by longing;
she reads and reads, fear rising.
But it often appears to me as if
she's taking elaborate pains
to hurt herself more accurately.
Deep in my heart, these things
just don't interest me:
the indiscriminate effects
of time. How the worst can happen.
So many things will lie
unrealized, that's the math.

The way she links things together
only brings out the violence.
Some of our perfect nights
you can't put into words.
And certain kinds
of defeat, they just keep you
talking through your hat.

BENT LYRE

I would bring out the coffee,

bread and butter, salt, and a piece of fruit.

The pigeons ran around in berserk patterns outside.

Our warm, clandestine complicity had the force of a new actuality.

Many mornings, we drank our coffee without any pleasantries.

At the table, along an axis of real and imaginary numbers, you made

your notes. I loved how true the imaginary numbers could be;

it was much more interesting than life—you could have company

and you could have loneliness in it. Your hardness

and your terrifying honesty could be bitter, but I forgave

the bitterness. Whenever we finally looked up from the clatter of small

cups and spoons, it was always near late afternoon. No decisions to make.

PASTORAL x 2

Drinks on the sunny patio, a hotel room key slipped
into a little envelope, fruit like flowers, flowers like birds,
and though at the time I could not understand
what he was saying, the sentiment landed, and it was like
a head hitting the stone tiles of that patio;
my temperament was blinked wide-awake,
like those birds-of-paradise with gaping orange beaks.

Later, I heard that the cat got inside, and the singing canary
was chewed up. I was standing in the kitchen at the time;
I thought of how dark and cold summers could be.

CLASSICS

Actaeon turns into a stag, I say, as I spear the fourth
       oily olive on my toothpick. He saw her nakedness, which was
appalling in the way it tested the air around it.

Then come the hounds, with their complicated names, the baying
       and the lurid viscera. Down this road we can scarcely follow in
   words, *theme — outlines?*
but I always feel the clothes newly on her back, and the low

calm that comes when bad temper is spent. He is inhumanly excited.

                                no return
A rack of antlers emerges from his forehead as I talk; there's no
       stuffing it back in. He doesn't seem to notice, as he pulls me into
   his lap.
I sip my drink, and the bartender decants striped red straws

               ×2
with their determined gaiety into a glass jar, carefully wipes down
       the scarred tabletop. Humiliation, what of it? Formerly, I had a few
feathers around my mouth, but nothing in my head.

PORTRAIT IN SUMMER

This floral swimsuit
is snarling. I am regularly spoiling
for a fight.
Within me, fat is always curing \o\
like a ham in a shed.

I go inside and read another psychosexual story ✓
set in a dreary seaside town:
there are water crossings, one too many
four-poster beds. Summertime: parole for academics.
Long days, low yields.

The flies stream into the kitchen,
bringing friends, spouting aphorisms:
the only major mystery left to life
is death. I prop an ashtray
on my bared stomach.

I should grow thinner, more of less
of me, as I grow more solitary.
But I haven't yet found   *theme — how much the body*
a manner in which to get over   *takes up space*
my inconsistencies.

On my way to fulfill
some banal commission, I'm conscious
of waiting for the season
to run its course,
and of accumulating an anger

around a simple truth:
all perfect friendships
eventually come to an end. Is it a story
that must at all costs
be dragged from the darkness?

It starts to rain, and the streets smell
like hot dogs, old pennies. The coffee shop
owner barely lifts his head from
the register as I approach the counter that's crowded
with menorahs, crosses, and Buddhas.

I meant to bring him a statue
of Venus de Milo for good measure.
It would all have the mixed effect of a moral
dullness and deep fear. I notice this is the only
place in town without a television.

I like the angry pinch of an insight; the rough
grasp of hard news. Yet in these
very dog days, what might have been ennobling
has often left me dull and vicious—
a surprise I just wasn't on to.

BARKING NOISES

Then he hated her. She had been farther
than he had. She led a nasty mental life. Her heart
always thumped like a stick dragged down the stairs.
The cat in the hallway rose
from its ersatz bed, quietly leading
its feminine life.
All three clocks in the apartment
pointed to half-past four
when he left. No one disbelieved the clocks. *authority*
She sat at the kitchen table
until the windows got dark. She dipped
a cold chicken drumstick into a saucer of salt
and ate it. It was delicious.

NAXOS

Nothing consummates an idyll
like abandonment.

Zoom back. A marvel then,
to be here with you.
Nude like fruit, and motiveless.

The gray-leaved olive trees outside seem like
young women: small, light, exciting.

I love you, I wish there was some more
original way of saying it.

We drink our bitter coffees on the terrace.
And the little dark stone
of work that secures me, where is it?

Millions of hard stars flood the sky
each night, gentle wording
defending mystery.

My own timidity, pale as meal,
will turn out to hold some ruthlessness, too.

I draw a line down the middle
of my life—   *wow!*
that's my night now, that's my day.

Each day the sea is blue, then amber,
then burning red; it declares love, it takes it back.

ENDINGS

The story has two endings.   *alternatives —*

It has one ending   *a relationship*

and then another.

Do you hear me?

I do not have the heart

to edit the other out.

THE BEGINNING OF SPRING

All winter our house was warm and deaf.
I could just see the few white flowers
outside the window. A true happiness occurred.
Don't stand there now asking to be loved.

We could feel the thawing in the river,
low and guilty. I was still learning her particularity,
all the beautiful colors in her face, even as my arms
loosened dreamlike from around her.

It all happened as my premonition told me it would. *back to fever dream*
I loved her, but I'm not sure she loved me back.
I know that many times I misspent
her hope: it was flowering, and it was finite.

Then again, maybe I'll want a young wife
in my old age. A bad man is the sort of man
who admires innocence. It's a theme that breaks her heart,
but not the one that's particularly unbearable.

I could touch her at any time. All the while
she was thinking of the work she wanted to do, despite
her absolute, unreasoning devotion to me. How life surprises you.
I had never been here before and yet I thought I understood it all.

What happens to old love, tell me if you know.

a finished relationship?
stuck in present – future?

✶THAT ARE

Then I became this stupid, trilling thing:
what I desired was to become obscene.

All the things I had loved up to then
fell away in the long struggle between winter and spring.

And then there was my body, inside of my soul.
It had different aspirations.

What form does it take without the soul?

Helpless in a hideous new way,
and as patient as a mountain. The soul is an innocent before it.

So when I say stupid, I simply offer meaninglessness.
And when I say trilling, I only mean a leaving off of past sound.

And when I am obscene, I am shorn of all expository passages.
And so on and so on, with things that are.

SPINOZA SAYS

He who loves God   *interesting choice of verb*
cannot endeavor that God
loves him in return.

Do you know,
I think the cool silver
of this is hard to live by.

When there is anything
you want very much,
you are making up a story   *metapoetics —*
                wow
all of the time,
of how you will get it
and how it will be.

You want the love of God
and the human sort. A big treasure
and a little treasure.

I wonder if you're like me,
a touch affronted by your own
underlying avidity.

For now, it is pleasant to lie
on one's bed, chronicling
everything in ice.

Though the hyenas in the room
and the real flowers, these things take
some of the innocence out of the day.

Want in a person
is like hunger in a dog, Spinoza
probably would not say.

His wakeful, solitary   nice ads
reasoning plainly outstrips
my wildest intuition.

Yet insofar as my heart
is a boot with a hole in it, I think
this is what writing could be

—what he calls Nature,
an existence no longer borne
as means or ends.

SAN FRANCISCO ✻ *like a railroad apt, but also like an inevitability*

My older neighbor on Rose Street once showed me
the contents of his rent-controlled apartment, just up the stairs from mine.
He was a hoarder, living in a state of tragic grandeur
that his circumstances did not entirely support.
Recurringly, his latest boyfriend would flee from him.
When we met later in the alley to take out the trash, we would reliably
turn into two lumps of fear. What was more terrifying than
being abandoned? Downstairs, I was a collector, too,
with my need to interpret and sort everything.
But we didn't tire of the spectacle
of our private lives, though many initiatives went badly wrong.
I was altogether more anxious about being light-minded.
My railroad apartment was a small cloth diary
with a lock and key. It was my real life,
or what so often passes among us for real life. And for all his possessions,
my neighbor dreamed of having a Petit Trianon with a vast garden
to walk in and dog roses lavishing a limitless dining room table.
Of course, there was no table, because there was no dining room.
Obviously, there was never a garden to walk in. *wow!*

more & more narrative — collector mind vs.
interpreter/sorter mind

Keat's Negative capability —
being okay w/ simply wrestling +
interrogation

43

REFUSENIKS

Her favorite person Flaubert says, When you

write the biography of a friend, you must do it

as if you were taking *revenge* for him. Who says

we have to live like everyone else? She drops a line down

onto the page: *In a poet's household, some people secretly love*

bad news. Like a dog in the kitchen, she investigates this scrap.

It could be a nod from Naturalism to Realism,

or a salute the other way around. It could be just

the sort of thing one writes when one feels

the stirrings of happiness close at hand.

THE ABSOLUTIST*

My grandmother ran her own business in Seoul,
an average, yet busy lunchtime canteen near the center
of the city. I can see her waiting for beverage deliveries, scrubbing down
sticky tables, enduring the smell of ripe garbage in the summers.
She always emerges from the building late in the day, dark and slim,
and walks home like someone floating down the Nile.
She took up with a careless, married man while death
was eating up most everything around her.
No one can tell me if it was a love match or if this was frankly
a more pragmatic way to live. I like to think she read whatever she wanted
while she ate alone, that she was thrilled with the stillness
at the end of her nights. I daydream that she was an enchanted, yet distracted
mother; she died soon after having her last child.
In every photo she turns away from the camera; cover anyone's face
and changed circumstances take up the burden of narrative.
She was said to be guiltily pretty and took chances; maybe she was
shallow. I tend to believe she was clear with herself, that
she was never worn away. I never can picture the food itself at all.

· tension of imagined life vs. reality
related to Something means Everything

SUMMER TERROR ·

I have never known much about flowers.
I can smell something on them,
such that I want to cry;
because like all flowers they look like ideas.
Their sensuality has never been thwarted;
no one remains inaccessible to them.
Though after nine nights must come ten,
in the everlasting tribunal of the garden.
So perhaps the flowers will now speak of me—
and tell of what it is like to be vivid with ants,
or prettily inscribed with red icing,
or held fast by envy, a net stiff with blood.

A WALK ROUND THE PARK ✦

We did not say much to each other but
we grinned,
      because this love was so good you sucked the
rib bones

and I licked my fingers like a cat.
Now I'm
      omniscient. I'm going to skip past *wow*
the hard

parts that go on for a very long time. Here's the
future:
      I laugh, because the pleasure was earned
yet vouchsafed,

and I made room for what was dead past and what
yet didn't
      exist. I was not always kind, but I
was clear.

multidirectional relationship — unknowing which way to face, to brace against

A SHAGGY DOG STORY — *long meandering story*

1.

I am hot and tiny,
yet I wrote *Jane Eyre*.

I died on a rainy Thursday
in Paris.

Much later, I come home to a household laid waste
by a tin of fatal corned-beef.

I take my pen name
from a small French village; I drink like a fish.

I'm always looking at the same piece
of paper, giving up hope and working a little.

What does art know? Sometimes it remarks,
I didn't think you were like that.

I thump my casing without feeling:
too much material,

and the steady hubbub within
seems off the point.

All this is a pig of an undertaking,
just to touch thoughts.

No one knows anything about
life's meaning—

Though it all gets carted away, even the great
scheme of things.

2.

In the middle of my life,
I felt a heave of something like nausea:

my real life had really begun,
no longer a speculative existence; though I still loved
having a whole day ahead of me.

Hurt and excited,
I wanted to get everything down
on the page.

I was as anxious to entertain
as Scheherazade, and as certain that if I failed,
I would die.

It seemed that anything less than that
was unfair.

3.

I saw my friends fall in love, their tremendous

happiness, deciding upon something at the last minute.

I pictured myself eating dirt.

My moods were like conspirators in an opera,

then strange-faced, like a jury. The view

from inside was nothing but walls and drainpipes

and a little sky. Florid eighteenth-century music against

taciturn furniture. And there was just me and my human concerns.

4.

I fell asleep thinking heaven is

renters in urban apartments, *places one might dwell in —*

the sanctioned anonymity sharpening

whatever's funny or jabbing in a person,

or misapplied or ruined.

Our likeability having nothing to do

with the legitimacy of our demands for privacy.

We bandaged up the bleeding and tearful young woman

from the first floor without comment on a Wednesday.

I think she went to the movies about an hour later,

looking as fresh as a daisy.

The steadying and flushed sensation of setting forth!

Whatever spring didn't restore,

you sometimes felt you could, with nothing left over.

5.

Love was losing its explanatory
power,

unromantic

wow! me too

      and I was beginning
to smell a rat.

Are we going to keep to this one
grand concern,

      like a serious drinker who sticks
to one drink?

      Start again.

Like all ideas, it appears to root
and come into leaf:

      the transience intensifies the effects,
sometimes it even flourishes in dryness.

Metaphors like this can be lazy,
and I am trying

      to get at the work of the matter.
The gap that is shaped like a person, the longing

to be with and to be alone, you give time
to all these things.

It goes on till all hours
        and somebody must clean up afterward;

then the silence begins wonderfully, wonderfully.

6.

Why must I urge you to feel the smallness of your life?
—I think it's a pleasure of the mind, like any other.

yeah, how a life is replicated on the page...

I think there must be a way to care for dogs
without treating them like dumb humans;
though the mind is one long unbreakable leash.

The other day, my friend declared that she favored
straightforward narratives: clear, unassuming, and if tart,
amiably so. I felt the reproach.

But style, as Diana Vreeland says, helps you
get down the stairs.

7.

Several months now passed
without event, several
years.

The grubs and worms themselves
tell the story, couriers
with few adjectives.

I think I have some capacity for abstract
reasoning, after
the world cools its details.

But I'm still having difficulty writing about time;
it does not appear to be the great healer
that all of us say it is.

8.

And here, life is going on, too:
a coffee pot, four towels, a book,
a lamp, and a bed.

Your ignorant hair grows long, you become drowsy
with lust, with infinite dogginess.

Pleasure!
Like a focusing lens.

You admire the bold loneliness of a real life
as never before.

And when the world treats you well,
you sometimes come to believe
you are deserving of it.

9.

I am traveling back to childhood,

      I am going to the sea.

I will throw myself down
onto the rocks,

          down into the sea,

where there are no predispositions.

10.

I was face down again in the dark blue
mud

where the cold and rocks and glints and verdigris
tried to draw me

into the passionate logic of their work

It was just after my eighth birthday, it made me
shy

What are you doing down there, my parents asked me

They had prepared winter food—stew, crude vegetables,
mung beans

But I couldn't be persuaded

The days up to then had been like pearls on a string, one
No after another, until

one day they were like a fire spreading, arrogant but sociable

Part of what makes life shameful and exciting
is the fact of being gripped

by something true that you just barely intuit

I breathed in its complex scents

THE MOUNTAINTOP

In truth, you still expect to order your life
in peace; you continue to long for glamour and passion.

To guard against the destiny
you don't really know, you work furiously.

Pensive and unathletic as you are, you have
your own intricate schedule,

with your shopping bags and appointments.
You always forget you're a bag of blood.

In sleep, these things lose
their power over you.

Meaninglessness does to you
what it can. When you wake, you have no ideas;

the heart is momentarily light.
As you slip back into the days, you find

you haven't done with certain notions yet.
You read all the time, help yourself to a plate of oysters.

The dreams become fresh and astounding once more,
renewed by the drama of betrayal.

Even the self you take to be so real
falls away while you labor,

and the only stones left are the ones in your throat,
forgone things you have to get down fast

or else you'll choke. At last, you don't even know
what you feel for yourself.

The mountaintop: you can keep your books
and your music there. What's bad in one story

is good in another. Something has made you brave.
There is more to life than writing.

documenting
the (possible)
demise of a
relationship

APRIL

Showers overnight. Coffee on the desk,
Untasted, now cold.

The birds have been silent all morning.
But you still suppose

The world will bound toward you,
Opening its gardens and doors!

The pale, irregular blush of Winter Daphne
Spreads outside and upward.

You remember those times when passion takes
Hold, its thousand-mile scent

Going all through a body. Can you beat that.

You can see the flower starting up
In people,

First the stealth, then the dartingness,
All the while focused

On some complex task of its own.

HAPPINESS

In the dream, I got up early
And went out to shoot a rabbit, because
There was no meat for Sunday.
It was too cold, horses and birds were frozen solid.
Nevertheless, the landscape pleased the purist in me.
I put on skates to go out on the gray pond.
All the while, a low fever clung to me; it was
As acrid as piss, as sweetish.
So I knew I still wanted to be loved.
I had no reflection there, but then who could be
Reflected in ice? I cried in my bed.
Yet, no mistaking it, it was my season,
I prospered. I made endless figure-eights
In a strange night exhilaration. My appetite was good.

[handwritten annotation:] returns us to Something
Means
Nothing

NOTES

"Chicago" borrows the phrase "restless for crowds and lights and noise" from Edna O'Brien's *The Country Girls*.

"The Beginning of Spring" borrows the line "A bad man is the sort of man who admires innocence" from Oscar Wilde.

"The Absolutist" is for Nancy Lim.

ACKNOWLEDGMENTS

My thanks to the editors of the following publications, in which these poems first appeared.

The Account: A Journal of Poetry, Prose, and Thought: "Classics"
The Baffler: "The Protagonists"
Grand: "The Mountaintop"
Hampden-Sydney Poetry Review: "Naxos"
jubilat: "Theme and Variation," "Chanson Douce," and "Endings"
LEON Literary Review: "April"
The New Republic: "That Are"
The New York Review of Books: "Boston" and "Pastoral"
Pinwheel: "Chicago"
Pleiades: "The Absolutist"
Poem-a-Day: "A Walk Round the Park"
Poetry: "Jean Rhys"
Provincetown Arts: "Portrait in Summer"
Smartish Pace: "Black Box"
The Volta: "The Beginning of Spring"
The Yale Review: "Bent Lyre," "San Francisco," and "The Stronger"
Zócalo Public Square: "Spinoza Says"

I am so grateful to Louise Glück for reading, vision, and friendship. Thank you to my friends for helping me see the potential in my efforts at both art and life, and for believing in them: Ash Anderson, Ian Chang,

Maggie Dietz, Graham Foust, Morgan Frank, Sally Keith, Tanya Larkin, Joseph Legaspi, John Lurz, Katie Peterson, James Shea, Jenn Sim, Asali Solomon, Jared Stanley, Michelle Sullivan, Jennifer Tseng, and Dorothy Wang. Thank you to the great team at W. W. Norton, in particular to Jill Bialosky and Drew Weitman for their care and editorial guidance. I thank the American Academy of Arts and Letters, my students and fellow writers at Warren Wilson College, and my colleagues at the University of Massachusetts Lowell, for encouragement and community. To my sister, Sharon, and my parents: thank you everlastingly for your blind love and trust.